COMPACT DISC PAGE AND BAND INFORMATION

MMO CD 4121

Music Minus One

Days Of Wine & Roses

Music Minus One Alto Saxophone

The Days Of Wine And Roses

BAND 1

Alto Sax

HENRY MANCINI
Arr. by Bob Wilber

MMO CD 4121

Bari. Lead

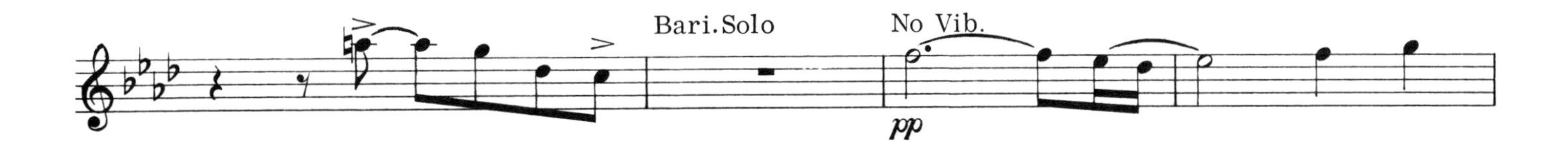
Bari. Solo
No Vib.
pp

3
Sopr. Lead
f

Unison
3
ff

3
Sopr. Lead

Sopr. Solo
2
cresc.

Play 3 times
1. 2.
3.
mp

Moon Mist

BAND 2
Alto Sax
MERCER ELLINGTON
Arr. by Bob Wilber
♩ = 54
Piano Intro.
Sopr.
Bari. Lead
Piano Solo
ppp
Alto
Flute Lead
to Clar.
Clar.
Alto
Clar.
To Alto
Alto
Sopr. Lead
MMO CD 4121

Lead
3
3

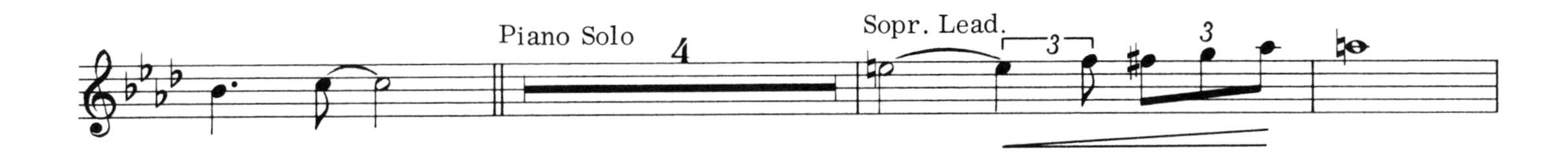
Piano Solo
4
Sopr. Lead.
3
3

Tenor Solo
ppp

3
cresc.

Sopr. Solo
3
3
3
3

Sopr. Solo
4
Bari. Lead

Acapulco Princess

BAND 3

Alto Sax

BOB WILBER

MMO CD 4121

pp
f
p
pp
Sopr. Solo
7
Sopr. Lead
3
Unison
Bari. Solo
p
2
Sopr. Lead
D. S. al Coda
CODA
rit.

MMO CD 4121

Two Moods For Piano And Winds

BAND 4

BOB WILBER

MMO CD 4121

Alto
3
Clar.
3

Alto
3
Piano Solo
Clar.
3
pp

2
mf
To Alto
2
Alto
mf

Sopr. Lead
3

3
3

3

mf
p

3
3
Piano Solo
To Clar.
7

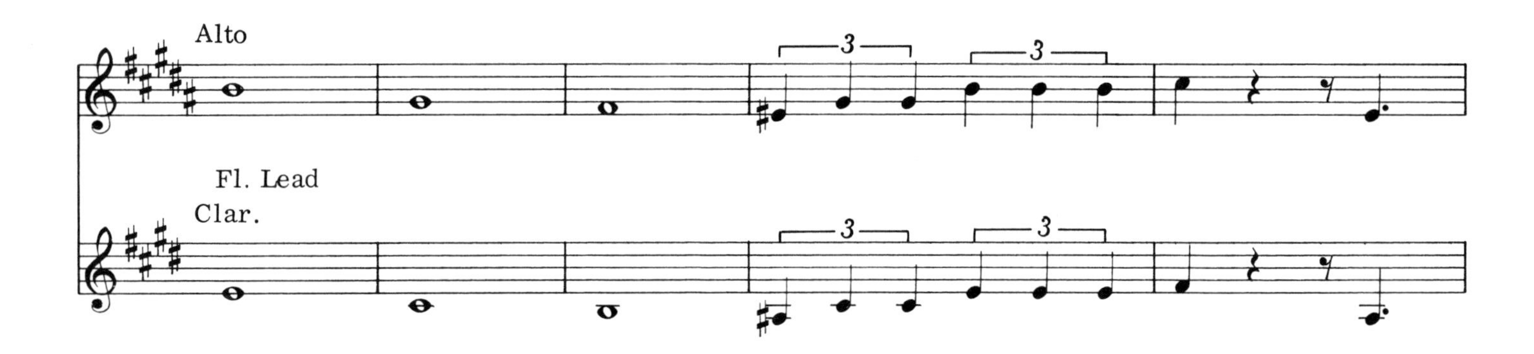
Alto
Fl. Lead
Clar.
3
3
3
3

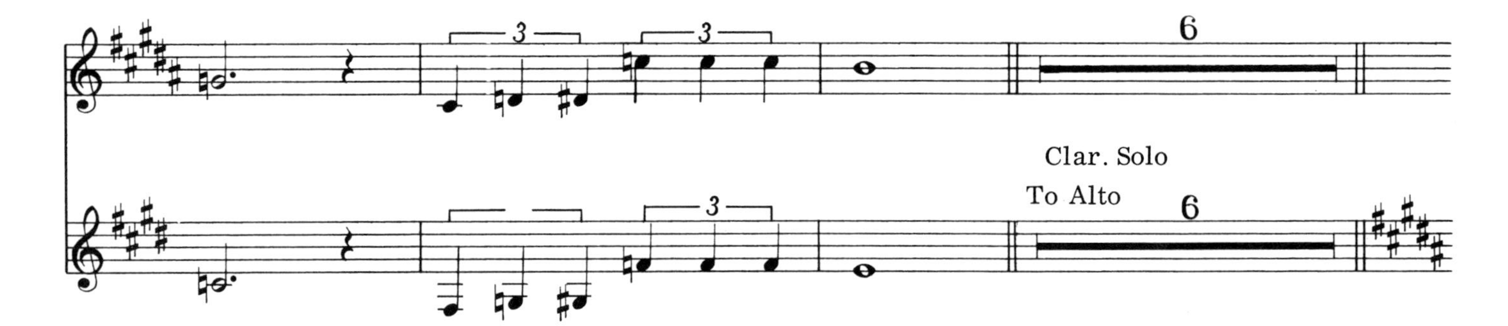
3
3
3
6
Clar. Solo
To Alto
6

Clar. Lead
Alto
mf
3
3
3
3

3
pp

The Mighty Hudson

BAND 5

Alto Sax

BOB WILBER

MMO CD 4121

Early Morning Blues

Alto Sax

BOB WILBER

MMO CD 4121

MMO MUSIC GROUP, INC., 50 Executive Boulevard, Elmsford, NY 10523-1325